SPUN

By Rabiah Hussain

‖SAMUEL FRENCH‖

Copyright © 2020 by Rabiah Hussain
All Rights Reserved

SPUN is fully protected under the copyright laws of the British Commonwealth, including Canada, the United States of America, and all other countries of the Copyright Union. All rights, including professional and amateur stage productions, recitation, lecturing, public reading, motion picture, radio broadcasting, television and the rights of translation into foreign languages are strictly reserved.

ISBN 978-0-573-13245-2

www.concordtheatricals.co.uk

www.concordtheatricals.com

FOR AMATEUR PRODUCTION ENQUIRIES

UNITED KINGDOM AND WORLD EXCLUDING NORTH AMERICA
licensing@concordtheatricals.co.uk
020-7054-7200

Each title is subject to availability from Concord Theatricals, depending upon country of performance.

CAUTION: Professional and amateur producers are hereby warned that *SPUN* is subject to a licensing fee. Publication of this play does not imply availability for performance. Both amateurs and professionals considering a production are strongly advised to apply to the appropriate agent before starting rehearsals, advertising, or booking a theatre. A licensing fee must be paid whether the title is presented for charity or gain and whether or not admission is charged.

This work is published by Samuel French, an imprint of Concord Theatricals.

The Professional Rights in this play are controlled by United Agents, 12-26 Lexington Street, London W1F 0LE

This work is published by Samuel French, an imprint of Concord Theatricals.

No one shall make any changes in this title for the purpose of production. No part of this book may be reproduced, stored in a retrieval system, or transmitted in any form, by any means, now known or yet to be invented, including mechanical, electronic, photocopying, recording, videotaping, or otherwise, without the prior written permission of the publisher. No one shall upload this title, or part of this title, to any social media websites.

The right of Rabiah Hussain to be identified as author of this work has been asserted in accordance with Section 77 of the Copyright, Designs and Patents Act 1988.

MUSIC USE NOTE

Licensees are solely responsible for obtaining formal written permission from copyright owners to use copyrighted music in the performance of this play and are strongly cautioned to do so. If no such permission is obtained by the licensee, then the licensee must use only original music that the licensee owns and controls. Licensees are solely responsible and liable for all music clearances and shall indemnify the copyright owners of the play(s) and their licensing agent, Concord Theatricals, against any costs, expenses, losses and liabilities arising from the use of music by licensees. Please contact the appropriate music licensing authority in your territory for the rights to any incidental music.

USE OF COPYRIGHT MUSIC

A licence issued by Concord Theatricals to perform this play does not include permission to use the incidental music specified in this copy. Where the place of performance is already licensed by the PERFORMING RIGHT SOCIETY (PRS) a return of the music used must be made to them. If the place of performance is not so licensed then application should be made to the PRS, 2 Pancras Square, London, N1C 4AG (www.prsformusic.com).A separate and additional licence from PHONOGRAPHIC PERFORMANCE LTD, 1 Upper James Street, London W1F 9DE (www.ppluk.com) is needed whenever commercial recordings are used.

IMPORTANT BILLING AND CREDIT REQUIREMENTS

If you have obtained performance rights to this title, please refer to your licensing agreement for important billing and credit requirements.

AUTHOR'S NOTE

I have always known I'm not white. But I didn't always know I was working class.

My earliest memory of racism is tied with home. At the age of six, my cousin and I stood silently in the front garden as the kids from a white family down the road strode past calling us "pakis". As they continued to walk away, we started conferring about what to call white people. When they reached their house, we shouted out "Engees!" – because English and white were interchangeable – whilst being ready to run inside should they decide this was a real insult. It was at that moment I understood "paki" to be a derogatory word for my skin colour, one that positioned whiteness into the centre of my wider view of the world.

Our response to being called "pakis" that day was a reflection of how we'd respond throughout our lives to the spotlight thrown on our identity. Not knowing the correct response to words used against us and fearing the reaction should we respond at all. The intimidation we'd always feel from the confidence of whiteness. Up until then I just looked different. But at that moment, I knew I wasn't white.

Realising I was working class came much later in my life, despite the fact that my identity has always been inextricably linked with home. I'm a Londoner through and through. But London to me has always been a vast estate, where those like me live in outhouses surrounding the extravagant mansion at the centre of it. This mansion is guarded by wrought iron gates that we can occasionally peer through but hardly ever enter. The white middle-class world within it was never visible to us from Newham, East London. Being a second-generation British Pakistani was the identity I attached to myself. The class element wouldn't come until I stepped through those iron gates and into that mansion.

Despite the Olympic and Westfield connection, most of Newham isn't like the London of TV and films. It's where immigrant communities have created a home away from home. Most people I knew growing up shared the same background and experiences as me – fathers working in factories, free school dinners and the majority of white faces around us were our school teachers. It's this shared experience that superficially sheltered many of us from what it means to be working class. Even when I went to sixth form in the slightly wealthier borough of Redbridge, sharing the same culture with the large South Asian population meant I still never thought of myself in terms of class. It also meant I didn't recognise racism either. It wouldn't be until I was much older that I'd realise the egg thrown at me by a white man in a white van was not a random act.

Stepping outside of East London, you start to see yourself in relation to wider structures. At university, I saw myself standing within the vast estate that is London, and in direct view of the mansion that was always inaccessible to me. Getting through university by doing admin roles in small offices felt like I had walked close enough to the iron gates to be able to look through them.

It was with my first job in a large organisation in central London that things changed. Walking past the lines of Asian shops on Green Street to get to Upton Park Station felt like approaching the iron gate that separated the outhouses, and travelling the district line was like walking towards the door of the mansion.

Getting off at St. James's Park and walking to the office, my entire world would change. I was standing in the mansion, scared to sit or touch the furniture. When you first enter this space, you feel invisible.

Being in a queue anywhere you are ignored as the white person behind you is served first. You are talked over, but all eyes are on you when there's a terrorist attack anywhere in the world. And you shrink. Partly because you felt invisible and partly because you stood out. In this mansion the cleaners, post room and canteen staff were mainly black, brown or Eastern European, whilst the majority of faces sitting at the computers were white. And I felt guilty for sitting amongst them.

I remember the exact moment I realised why I felt so out of place here. There were other people of colour who seemed to be comfortable, so what was wrong with me?

When an MP made headlines for criticising Oxford's quota system for minority and working-class students, I listened to the general debate amongst my colleagues. And the words of my boss are ones that I've never forgotten.

"I agree. I don't pay thousands of pounds for my kids to go to private school just so some smelly oik can take their place." The silence from others was indicative of what they felt about this comment. But the fact was no one there was from a working-class background. But for me it felt like the words were deployed against me. I was that smelly oik in the room. It's the first time I realised that I was working class.

I use the word deploy quite deliberately here, because the effect of language from those in more privileged positions is used without recognising the violence it can cause. Words don't always land on your body and fall off. They hit you like artillery fire. They seep into your bones. Words can shatter you. Even whilst writing this I can feel where those wounds were.

It's in order to heal these wounds that many of us try to shed what we can of our identities. People can see race but try hard enough and class can be hidden. You can change the way you speak, how you carry yourself, your viewpoints, all in the hope you'll neither be invisible nor too conspicuous. With this you try to adopt traits that are more white and middle class. And the most painful part – you start to look upon those outside the iron gates in a certain way because you want to disassociate yourself from them. You start to call the mansion home.

But identity is not so easy to erase. You can pack away parts of who you are but this space was never made for you and will always see you in a certain way. Words continue to land on you, breaking your bones. "Are you going to have an arranged marriage?", "Where are you really from?", "You're really different." Words can change your sense of self. When I tried desperately to wash and dry the only coat I owned when that egg was thrown at me, I didn't feel working class. But when privilege used the words "smelly oik", it took me years to recover. That is the reality of words. Microaggressions are delivered with a smile by those you normally consider "nice people", so it becomes difficult to know how respond to them, despite the rupture they cause internally once the words really sink in. It's a reminder of the confidence of whiteness I had experienced from childhood.

Rabiah Hussain, 2020

NOTES ON TEXT

'...' Indicates when a character is talking to another character

"..." Indicates when a character is voicing someone else in the story

/ Indicates an interruption

... Indicates a thought or pause

SPUN

Spun by Rabiah Hussain was first performed at the Arcola Theatre and ran for 30 performances between 27 June and 28 July 2018.

SAFA　　　　　　　　　　　　　　　　Humaira Iqbal
AISHA　　　　　　　　　　　　　　　　　Aasiya Shah

Writer　　　　　　　　　　　　　　Rabiah Hussain
Director　　　　　　　　　　　　　　Richard Speir
Designer　　　　　　　　　　　　　　Khadija Raza
Lighting Designer　　　　　　　　　　Geoff Hense
Sound Designer　　　　　　　　　　　Anna Clock
Movement Director　　　　　　　　　Nancy Kettle
Stage Manager　　　　　　　　　Catriona McHugh
Production Manager　　　　　　Philippa J. Robinson
Production LX　　　　　　　　Matthew Swithinbank
Assistant Director　　　　　　　　　Catriona Tait

WITH THANKS TO

Alex Defert, Aryana Ramkhalawon, Emily Ansorge, Fin Kennedy, Liz Hyder, Fozia Khaliq, KPMG, Lisa Goldman, Muddassar Ahmed, Nadi Kemp-Sayfi, Nic Connaughton, Rosamunde Hutt, Yasmeen Khan.

For Mum and Dad

CHARACTERS

SAFA – 21, British Pakistani, Londoner
AISHA – 21, British Pakistani, Londoner

PROLOGUE

AISHA 'What do you see when you look at me?'

SAFA 'Everything I don't want to be.'

Beat.

'What do you see when you look at me?'

AISHA 'Everything I shouldn't have been.'

ACT ONE

Lights go up.

SAFA *and* AISHA *on stage.*

SAFA Shit! She's here? Never early for anything, but the one day I need her to be late.

AISHA Made it! Send her a text. Tell her I'm outside and to hurry up 'cos I ain't here to wait around for her, you know. So stupid she makes me do this. Her mum's never gonna check up on her. Never has. But this one's extra cautious. Always has been.

Beat.

Why is she dangling her new brown boots at me from her bedroom window?

'What?'

Whatever the bitch's mouthing is going straight over my head. Might as well be doing sign language. Hold my thumbs up. Tell her,

'Boots are sick.'

Beat.

What's she mean 'no'? Why ask if she's decided not to wear 'em. Dickhead.

SAFA Oh, my days. Whoever said best friends can always understand each other, no matter what, was chattin' bare crap.

AISHA You know how girls have their boyfriends waiting around the corner for them? I get the privilege without having the goods.

SAFA This is exactly what living in a semi-detached is for.

AISHA She's holding out some blue carrier bag now. Think her boots are in it.

Beat.

Is she aiming towards where I'm parked?!

SAFA Basic projectile motion science here. There it goes...

AISHA What??

SAFA There it... No!

AISHA Idiot! That's the worst throw in the world. Trying to be bloody Shahid Afridi. I swear, once she has her mind set on wearing something, she just has to wear it. Queen fucking Victoria.

Whatever, I can't do nothing about it.

SAFA Run to the living room, fast as I can. Look round hoping to get a clear way to the back garden... but Mum's praying in front of the patio door!

Send Aisha a text.

'Beg you get 'em for me.'

AISHA Fuck's sake, how am I supposed to do that? Swear down, she really takes the piss.

Beat.

'Fine.'

SAFA 'Yes!'

AISHA 'But she owes me big time.'

SAFA Now, I can see that the bag has landed about two meters away, but Mum prays with her back to the door, so if she hurries...

AISHA Always been pretty athletic I have. The number of times I've out-run and out-climbed the police when they'd seen me bunking in Plashet Park. But this. This is real. Safa's Mum.

Here I go.

SAFA Best thing about mums at this time is, that no matter what's happening around them, they don't look up from their prayer. For anything.

AISHA One foot in the bit with a brick missing. I pull myself up and look over. I see them! See Safa's mum too, but only thing gonna distract her right now is the Judgement Day trumpet. One big jerk up, over and I land right on my feet. Proper Olympic shit.

SAFA I pretend I'm cleaning up. Side-eyeing the garden the whole time. She gets on her hands and knees and does some Rambo shit across the grass. Commando crawling and that. She's showing some mad skills right now.

She has the bag! She's getting ready to jump back over... But she ducks?

Beat.

Mum's finishing prayers! I can't look!

AISHA Fucking hell, get her out of there.

SAFA I ask Mum to show me the fabric she bought from Green Street. Try to lead her out of the room but she empties the bag right there!

AISHA Is this the time for the bitch to be checking out clothes?

SAFA I'm pretty sure I'm about to pass out any minute.

AISHA Fuck it.

SAFA She aims, fires, and the bag is over! She's taking one last look around, leaps up, hands on the wall and hurls herself back outside.

AISHA This time, I land straight on my arse.

SAFA She did it!

AISHA I'm a fucking G!

SAFA She'll be dancing around the car right now and banging on about this for days.

AISHA They should get me to represent team GB in 2012, innit.

Beat.

Ah, my fucking trainers, man! It took me ages to find these. Wish I'd been wiser choosing a best friend.

I get back in the car and I can tell you exactly how it's all happening in Safa's house right now.

SAFA *is doing exactly what* AISHA *is describing.*

She's gonna run upstairs to her room, change her top, put a jacket on so her mum can't see what she's wearing. Then she's gonna go back downstairs, wave bye, pretending she's off to uni but avoiding her mum's gaze 'cos Safa can't lie for shit, and just as she's about to leave the house, her younger brother's gonna wanna wrestle her for jokes, cos he knows she's really off somewhere else.

SAFA Little shit!

AISHA And any minute now… Yep, she runs like a fire is chasing her and flings herself in.

Beat.

SAFA 'Love ya.'

AISHA 'Fuck off.'

SAFA I'm ready to celebrate slash mourn the end of uni.

Beat.

'Ready?'

AISHA 'Doing this for you, bitch.'

Coloured lights and Bhangra music.*

SAFA 'Come on, dance!'

AISHA 'No, thanks.'

SAFA 'Fine, be boring.'

Beat.

AISHA Despite their age, the majority of girls here aren't allowed out past nine pm. But doesn't mean they don't want to rebel within boundaries. So, seizing the opportunity to provide a second best alternative, a bunch of DJ's and money minds set up Desi Nights... And they're shit. Whoever heard of clubbing at seven pm? I could've been getting ready for some sick rave right now. But instead...

SAFA I fucking love this! Lying to mum is shitty, I know. But I can't tell her that instead of learning about Henry Gantt, I'm dancing to the heavy beats of DJ Sanj.

AISHA Dad doesn't really lay down any rules for me. Gives me space so long as I'm not doing anything too outrageous. And trust me, this is no where near my definition of outrageous. 'Course, can't tell him I enjoy the occasional Jäger shot and the not-so-occasional Peroni. But at least I don't do drugs... Well, apart from the occasional spliff. But that's a grey area.

SAFA My strategy? Compartmentalise the guilt 'til I get back home. Then, along with the sparkly top, I change my act. And yes, the guilt kicks in when I see Mum, but I remind myself, I'm only dancing. No alcohol, no drugs, and definitely no grinding against the manky Asian boys who automatically assume you're easy just because you like to let your hair down...

---

* A licence to produce SPUN does not include a performance licence for any third-party or copyrighted music. Licensees should create an original composition or use music in the public domain. For further information, please see Music Use Note on page iii

AISHA ...And with clinical precision, seven minutes from entering, some knobhead starts coming towards me doing what looks like the chicken dance to Miss Dynamite. Trouble with the guys in East London is that they're all so fucking predictable.

"Alrite? What's your name?"

'Aisha.'

He looks down at the beer in my hand and nods his head like he's one of those Churchill bulldog toy things.

"Aisha? Are you Muslim?"

Dickhead smells like Bacardi Breezers and weed but has the balls to ask me that question? I stand up straight and square up to him.

'Fuck off back to your cave, mate.'

SAFA Not again.

AISHA He's about to walk off but before he does, under his breath,

"Fucking slag."

Nah, I ain't having that.

SAFA I stop her. For his sake not hers.

'Fuck it, you can't fight all the knobs.'

Lights change. AISHA *starts to light up a cigarette.*

AISHA 'One of these days you're gonna have to back me up.'

SAFA 'Just ignore them.'

AISHA 'People will walk all over you if you don't stand up for yourself.'

SAFA 'I can stand up for myself. Remember/ in...'

AISHA 'In/ first year when you had a go at Faiza for copying your essay. It don't count if you went and apologised later.'

SAFA 'How do you know that?'

AISHA 'I'll never understand why you need everyone to like you.'

SAFA 'I can't be like you, okay. Always looking for a fight.'

AISHA 'No. I just don't take shit.'

SAFA *notices* AISHA's *scuffed trainers.*

SAFA 'Owe you one.'

AISHA 'I ain't got the time to be climbing over walls for you. Your mum don't even say nothing to you.'

SAFA 'She'd keep calling to ask where I am.'

AISHA 'You know she's a worrier. Exactly like you are.'

SAFA 'She treats me like a baby.'

AISHA 'You literally ask her to feed you.'

SAFA 'Only when I'm tired!'

Beat.

'Our last moments of being students. Feels weird.'

AISHA 'Hm.'

SAFA 'Are you scared?'

AISHA 'About?'

SAFA 'Whatever's next.'

AISHA 'What's there to be scared of? You figure out what you want, and, you go for it.'

SAFA 'You know what I'm looking forward to the most? Being able to walk into a shop and buying stuff I want without stressing about money. And giving some to Mum and Dad. Contributing like you do.'

AISHA 'I only do a bit of shopping.'

SAFA 'I badly want that Marketing Associate job in central.'

AISHA 'You'll get it.'

SAFA 'Let's do something different for our birthdays' this year. Go somewhere fancy in central.'

AISHA 'You're gonna turn into one of them posh twats, aren't you?'

SAFA 'Swear down you have to ruin every plan I make. Fine, we'll just go Dixy or some shit.'

AISHA 'Okay, man. Somewhere fancy in central then.'

SAFA 'Don't do me any favours.'

AISHA 'I can't win with you.'

Beat.

SAFA 'What do you think we'll be doing in ten years time?'

AISHA 'Why ten?'

SAFA 'Just. Random.'

AISHA 'I don't know. I don't like this game.'

SAFA 'I think we'll still be tight /and'

AISHA 'Why /wouldn't we be tight?'

SAFA 'I said we will be.'

AISHA 'Yeah, but why would that even be a thought?'

SAFA 'It's not, man. I just said it. I think we'll still be tight and hang out all the time and...well, not all the time... Shit! Thursdays won't be our day anymore!'

AISHA 'Why?'

SAFA 'Cos of work.'

AISHA 'We can take the day off.'

SAFA 'It's not uni.'

AISHA 'When we gonna hang out then?'

SAFA 'I know! We'll meet outside Upton Park in the mornings and go to work together. And then come home together in the evenings.'

AISHA 'Don't need to see that much of you.'

SAFA 'Well, you won't if you haven't sent your application off still?'

AISHA '...'

SAFA 'Aisha! Deadline's next week. Samina and all them lot applied ages ago. The scheme's only for Newham, so do you know how many people from ends will be applying? Practically half our year is. I'll come over tomorrow and help you.'

AISHA 'Nah, it's fine.'

SAFA 'I know you, you'll leave it 'til the last minute. When I come /over...'

AISHA 'I'm /not applying, Safa.'

Beat.

SAFA 'Why not?'

AISHA 'I want to be there for Dad the next few months.'

SAFA 'What d'you mean?'

AISHA '...'

SAFA 'Oh.'

AISHA 'I just need a chilled out job for a bit. I'll apply next year.'

SAFA 'What are you going to do then? Stay part-time at New Look?'

AISHA 'No.'

SAFA 'Then?'

Beat.

AISHA 'I'm gonna be a TA.'

SAFA 'TA? What's that?'

AISHA 'Teaching Assistant, you idiot.'

SAFA *(laughs)* 'You're gonna be a teacher?'

AISHA 'No, Assistant! You know my cousin, Tara? She said to apply for her class and help in the science department.'

SAFA 'Bitch, that's our old school.'

AISHA 'It's just temporary. I ain't gonna be there long.'

SAFA 'But... you're gonna be shit.'

AISHA 'What the fuck, man?'

SAFA 'What d'you want me to say? You're not exactly a people person. And you hated school.'

AISHA 'I'll be the cool one. The girl's will love me.'

SAFA 'Yeah, alright.'

AISHA 'Thanks for the support.'

Beat.

SAFA 'Your mum would've been proud.'

AISHA 'That's not why I'm doing it, okay.'

SAFA 'That's not what I... Okay, I'm sorry. I think you'll be crap, but I hope I'm wrong.'

AISHA 'Bitch.'

Beat.

SAFA 'Do you realise it's the first time we're gonna be doing different things?'

Beat.

'I'm gonna miss you, man. The jokes we have.'

AISHA 'Don't get emotional. You know I can't deal with that shit.'

SAFA 'Fine. Stupid cow.'

Beat.

AISHA She's an idiot. But I do love her.

SAFA Glued to each other, our teachers always said. But she's fine on her own.

Beat.

AISHA 'Evenings.'

SAFA 'What?'

AISHA 'We'll meet Thursday evenings. Every week.'

SAFA 'Yes! Dinner and sheesha?'

AISHA 'Whatever.'

SAFA 'Love you.'

AISHA 'Fuck off.'

Lights change.

SAFA Aisha drops me off home. When I get inside, my brother is sleeping and mum and dad are watching Geo TV.

Beat.

Mum's left dinner for me on the kitchen table. Doesn't matter what time I get home, she always does that.

AISHA Dad's sleeping, but like every night, he leaves a glass of milk for me on the counter. Like mum used to for him.

Beat.

Her picture sits on the mantelpiece. I've always hated having it there. I hardly ever look at it.

Beat.

I've never told him I hate milk.

Lights change.

Helping Tara teach secondary to me was supposed to be like, Dead Poet's Society. Or at least I could be the cool one, like Jack Black, finding talent for something or other. But I'm hardly past the school gates and already I can tell that these girls are absolute arseholes.

SAFA Woke up well early! Couldn't sleep 'cos of the excitement. I'm on the District Line and as we go past each stop, I notice how everything changes. From Upton Park, Plaistow, Mile End to Monument. The faces, the clothes, the way people talk. Even though it's English, it morphs from *ghetto* into the *Queen's English*. But one thing is the same. Everyone looks fucking miserable.

AISHA They're running around throwing water on each other! One splashes me on the arm and little shit doesn't even stop. Shouts, "sorry!" and legs it. I'm sure we weren't as bad as these lot.

Beat.

Well...

SAFA I love London. Always have. Ever since that first trip to the Science Museum in school. The buildings, travelling by tube, the rush. Even the tourists!

Beat.

I get my MP3 player out. Aisha's made me a sick playlist for my journey.

Garage blasts until it abruptly stops and a cheesy Bollywood song[*] comes on. SAFA *panics, quickly changes it, hoping no one on the train heard it.*

Stupid cow!

---

[*] A licence to produce SPUN does not include a performance licence for any third-party or copyrighted music. Licensees should create an original composition or use music in the public domain. For further information, please see Music Use Note on page iii.

AISHA Tara's showing me around the Science lab like I didn't spend five years in this school. Me and Safa used to sit in that corner over there.

She's on some next flex now saying all this will look good on my PGCE application. Tell her, 'I'm not doing a PGCE!' Saved by the bell as the kids start coming in.

I sit at the back of the class, notepad and pen ready.

That brat who threw the water on me walks in. Tries to hide behind her friend. But I seen her.

SAFA Kim, my boss, collects me from reception. We get the lift up and she's telling me about the scheme. Permanent job if I smash my review!

We get off at the fifteenth floor and the view is beautiful. All the people outside look like ants from up here.

AISHA The little brat's name is Sadia. I swear I ain't about to be wound up on my first day, but Tara ain't looking and she's jumped on my table, is leaning over me and changing the clock to get out of class early.

Beat.

I'm right here! But she thinks I'm invisible 'cos I'm not actually a teacher. Plenty of detentions if I decide to tell Tara. Just watch.

SAFA Kim takes me around the floor introducing everyone. I'm trying to remember names but all I can notice is how posh and that everyone speaks. Like the words are, like, long and tall.

(posh voice) "Welcome to the team, Safa."

I imagine their necks being as stiff as a giraffe's, that's the only way the words can come out like that.

AISHA The one place we were never allowed to go and today, I'm in the staff room, man! Tara's making me do a shit load of photocopying. I swear I didn't sign up to be her servant.

Beat.

Out of the window, I can see the bus stop where me and Safa used to wait when we'd bunk off. She hated bunking, but was so easy to convince her.

SAFA My desk is sick! I organise my pens in a straight line. Opposite me sits Tim. I'm trying to concentrate but I'm too distracted by him having a polite verbal dissing match with someone. The guy walks off and Tim just tuts. His version of giving the finger. I can't wait to tell Aisha!

AISHA Shit, Miss Crankshaw, my old form tutor. I hide my face but she sees me and comes over. She's telling Tara about all the dumb shit I used to do. I side step away and start stapling the photocopies. I'm counting down to the next class.

Never thought I'd say that.

SAFA I've spoken as little as possible the entire day. I'm scared I'm going to blurt something out like,

'Yeah, that was such a *bad* – as in good – episode wasn't it?'

Right now, Tim is cracking a joke about the CEO. The whole team's in fits and I'm about to put into practice what I've seen is the best response to a joke in the office. Instead of saying, 'that's sick', I say, 'That is brilliant!' My tallest voice, even though I don't understand what the fuck is so funny about someone choking on their Weetabix. But still. I'm well proud of myself. Innit.

Beat.

Oh, my god. An Asian person! We both notice each other!

AISHA I'm obviously not invisible anymore.

"Aisha. Aisha."

They pretend they're calling the Aisha sat in the front of the class. Idiots! Last bell rings and I run to get my arse home. These corridors are taking me back to school days. Weird being here without Safa though.

SAFA I pack up to go home. Helen is adding a new picture to her desk. Here, desks are decorated like they're bodies stamped with personalities. Always telling you something about the person who sits there. Pictures of families on skiing holidays, coffee cup stains and gym bags everywhere. A world apart from pictures of Quran passages, holidays to Pakistan and maybe a wedding in Middlesbrough.

Beat.

I love having my own desk. But I haven't decided which personality it will take yet.

Lights change. A Thursday. SAFA's *bedroom.*

'What earrings go with this?'

AISHA 'Hoops.'

SAFA 'Hoops? I don't wanna look like an East London girl, you know.'

AISHA 'Why not?'

SAFA 'Cos everyone dresses all proper and that... I need to get some studs.

Beat.

Did you hear about Samina? She got a job in a company down the road from me. We're going for lunch tomorrow.'

AISHA 'She's so boring.'

SAFA 'You can still apply directly to places, you know?'

AISHA 'Don't start. Been getting it from Tara about doing a PGCE too.'

SAFA 'Then look for something in central. You're hating school anyway.'

AISHA 'Think I'll hate the posh twats you talk about even more. Anyway, can't be bothered to fill out application forms.'

SAFA 'So lazy. Still can't believe you got a first.'

AISHA 'Gifted, innit. But two one is good too. Not as good as a first but still.'

SAFA 'Cow.'

Beat.

'Hey, they're announcing the Olympics day before my birthday. If we get it, let's go Trafalgar Square.'

AISHA 'What's happening in Trafalgar Square?'

SAFA 'Celebrations, obviously. Some of my work lot are going.'

AISHA 'Why'd you want me there then?'

SAFA 'It'll be fun... I just thought I'd *run it up the flagpole.*'

Beat.

AISHA 'Excuse me?'

SAFA 'I'm just *bringing a new idea to the table.* You know, *thinking outside the box* a bit. Or am I just *flogging a dead horse with you?*'

AISHA 'Can you speak English!'

SAFA *(laughing)* 'That's how they talk in meetings. My jaw is hurting from trying to talk all posh. I have to laugh along to jokes I don't get either.'

AISHA 'Well, leave that posh twat stuff in the office. I don't wanna hear it.'

SAFA 'I swear they go for drinks at the pub like every day.'

AISHA 'Why don't you go?'

SAFA 'They might ask why I don't drink.'

AISHA 'Tell them to mind their own fucking business. And don't go being pressured into drinking or anything. I know you. You'll feel guilty.'

SAFA 'You going to come with me or not?'

AISHA 'They're gonna be in our manor so why is everyone celebrating in Trafalgar Square?'

SAFA ''Cos they're the London games.'

AISHA 'Then they be should be celebrating where the games are gonna be happening. Here. The real London.'

SAFA 'How is Trafalgar Square not the *real London*? Where d'you think all the tourists go?'

AISHA 'Wherever the travel guides tell them to, and that ain't Forest Gate.'

SAFA 'Have you forgotten what Forest Gate looks like?'

AISHA 'Lots of shops called *Choudhary & Sons*. No, I haven't forgotten.'

Beat.

'Have you even told your work lot that Stratford is down the road from you?'

SAFA 'I was about to but then they all started talking about which sports they played in school and stuff. I thought they were talking about in PE lessons. But one of them was in a professional hockey team. They all did like track, rowing, tennis, rugby. All I have is playing cricket in the back garden with my cousin's. So I just stayed quiet.'

AISHA 'Tell them you're Asian. You learnt to sprint whenever you ran from your mum. The posh twats might not understand but whatever.'

SAFA 'Why d'you keep calling them that?'

AISHA 'Cos they're posh twats. I mean, who the hell does rowing?'

SAFA 'I'm serious. I don't like it.'

AISHA 'Why you getting so defensive? Not like you know them properly.'

SAFA 'And you don't know them at all, so don't know why you keep judging them.

You know what, forget coming central. God knows what you're going blurt out if we see them.'

AISHA 'I won't say anything.'

SAFA 'Yeah, you will. You can't help it.'

AISHA 'Okay, fine. I'll keep my mouth shut. I promise! I'm even agreeing to come.'

Beat.

SAFA 'Fine. Love you.'

AISHA 'Fuck off.'

Lights change.

SAFA We gather around the TV screen in the office. Everyone is buzzing. Pin drop silence.

Beat.

We did it! London will be hosting the 2012 Olympics!

AISHA Festival atmosphere in school. I don't know whether they're excited about the Olympics or the fact that Tara is letting them have a free lesson, but the girls are buzzing.

SAFA Kim suggests a lunch to celebrate. A Portuguese Restaurant near the station. The closest I've had to Portuguese food is Nando's! I look up the menu. Google the things I don't know. Yep, I'm gonna be ready for this.

AISHA The whole school gathers in the playground at lunch to play sports. Sea of young Asian girls excited over something they're not even involved in.

Mr James, the PE teacher, tells me to hand out tennis balls. 'That's not even my job!' Tara gives me the *you better* look. He throws the bag of balls at me and walks off. Idiot.

SAFA I stop at the cash machine on the way to the restaurant. My first pay day today. Growing up was mainly free school dinners and wearing the same coat for three winters. But today, I've earned the money myself.

I insert my debit card, punch the pin in, hold my breath, praying I didn't give them the wrong account details. Check balance. Wait. Wait. Yes! I feel like Miss Independent.

AISHA Walking around like a chump handing out tennis balls and none of them even notice me.

Beat.

Tara looks more like their friend than their teacher right now. They're having bare jokes.

SAFA Shit, it's packed! We're going to a Japanese restaurant instead. I know nothing about Japanese food! *Daikon Salad... Tempura... Tataki*? Panic takes over as I listen to what others are ordering. I stumble over words when Helen asks me what I want. She gives me a warm smile and explains the different dishes. I thank her.

Beat.

I miss home all of a sudden.

AISHA Safa must be bare happy right now.

Lights change.

SAFA I wait for Aisha outside the office with Kim, Tim, and Helen chatting about the Olympics. I'm about to tell them that I live in Newham when Tim says, "Lucky I used to run track. Never know when you'll be mugged around there."

Beat.

They all laugh.

AISHA I walk out the station towards her office. I turn the corner and I can see Safa standing outside with a bunch of people. They look deep in conversation. I'm hoping she will say bye before I get there.

SAFA Then Kim jumps in.

"Hope they get rid of all the *smelly oiks* by 2012, eh Safa?"

Beat.

Smelly oiks? I don't respond. And I can't seem to bring myself to say anything. And the others keep laughing...

She's shocked to see AISHA *behind her.*

(surprised) 'Aisha?!'

AISHA 'Hey.'

SAFA *(nervously)* 'When did you get here?'

AISHA 'Just now.'

SAFA I pray she didn't hear that. I quickly say bye.

(posh voice) 'Have a lovely evening all. See you tomorrow.'

Beat.

'Shit. You're never going to let me live that down are you.'

AISHA 'No, I'm not. *(posh voice)* Sa-fa.'

SAFA Kim and them are starting to make their way, not far behind. I don't want them to catch up.

'Can we get coffee.'

AISHA 'Since when do you drink coffee?'

Beat.

We're waiting near the counter and some white dude, tall, pretty fit, starts talking to us. Well, to her mainly. I don't get any of his jokes, so I stay quiet.

SAFA "And, er, where are you guys from?"

I tell him we're from East London.

AISHA You know he wants to hear India or something.

SAFA 'Our parents are from Pakistan but we were born here.' He nods his head.

"That makes sense. You both look very contemporary?"

Beat. Both laugh.

AISHA I'm guessing he's referring to the Starbuck's cups in our hands because I don't know what the fuck that means. He tries to impress us with his knowledge of Pakistan. Says

"Namaste". Making the mistake of getting the country, language and religion wrong. Safa's too nice to tell him to shut up, so I make an excuse and get us out of there.

'What a knob.'

SAFA 'He was just being friendly.'

Beat.

AISHA We get out onto Trafalgar Square and the crowd is insane. Summer heat is perfect today. Like a proper big, noisy party. Flags and balloons all over the place. News crews and cameras. People drinking and dancing. Even I'm liking it.

But on the train home, Safa's bare quiet.

Lights change.

'How come you don't correct your colleagues about your name?'

SAFA 'What do you mean?'

AISHA *'Sa-fa*? They're saying it wrong.'

SAFA 'Not a big deal. It was the same with teachers in school and uni and stuff. They just pronounce it different.'

AISHA 'So? Tell them that.'

SAFA 'Can't go around correcting everyone all the time can I.'

Beat.

AISHA 'Safa, you're okay, right?'

SAFA 'Yeah. Why?'

AISHA 'You'd tell me if something is bugging you, or if someone has said anything.'

SAFA 'You know I will.'

AISHA 'Good.'

SAFA 'Why are you asking though?'

AISHA 'Just. No reason.'

Beat.

SAFA 'It's nothing. Just that we went to this restaurant for lunch. I didn't have a clue what anything was.'

AISHA 'So what? You're trying things out. That's the point, right?'

SAFA 'Yeah, but I felt so out of place. Helen had to help me order.'

AISHA 'Bet that made her feel good. Posh twat teaching you something.'

SAFA 'I told you before I don't like you calling them that.'

Beat.

AISHA 'Okay, sorry. If it helps, I'm feeling same at work. No one even notices me.'

SAFA 'At least you won't be there for long.'

Beat.

AISHA 'Yeah.'

Beat.

'Got you something!'

SAFA 'My birthday's tomorrow.'

AISHA 'I'm gonna give you the *real* present then.'

Hands her a small box.

SAFA 'Studs!'

AISHA 'You can look all proper and that.'

SAFA 'Thank you.'

Beat.

AISHA 'Listen, pull a sickey tomorrow. We can hang out.'

SAFA 'Aisha. I have to work.'

AISHA 'But we always spend birthdays together.'

SAFA 'We are.'

AISHA 'No, after work isn't the same. The full day.'

SAFA 'You're supposed to be in school aren't you?'

AISHA 'They won't miss me. Come on. Just call in the morning and say you're ill.'

SAFA 'I can't. I'm gonna feel bad.'

AISHA 'You didn't need much convincing in uni.'

SAFA 'This isn't uni.'

AISHA 'Please!

(points at her trainers) And you still owe me, remember? Look how long it's been since we hung out properly. Like we used to.'

Beat.

'Come on.'

Beat.

SAFA 'Swear, you always do this to me.'

AISHA 'Yes! I'll pick you up in the morning.'

SAFA 'Fine.'

AISHA 'Love me?'

SAFA 'Fuck off'

Lights change. The next day.

AISHA I wake up later than I should've. Make myself a cup of tea, toast and sit down for some Channel U and Flava. In the mood for some two-step and Grime. I'm doing my usual flicking through the channels.

Beat.

Fuck.

Beat.

Bomb attacks in London.

Beat.

I've never really seen central as home before. But today. London is...

SAFA ...London.

AISHA I send Safa a message. She ain't replying.

Beat.

What if she went to work?!

SAFA I can't move from the TV. Mum's getting phone calls to ask if I'm okay. She keeps thanking God that I didn't go into work today.

Beat.

I wish she'd stop saying that.

AISHA I get to her house and knock on the door repeatedly. Her Mum answers.

'Safa?!'

Beat.

She tells me Safa's fine.

I walk in and I'm about to close the front door behind me when my phone buzzes. A message from Safa?

I take a few steps through the hallway.

Beat.

I can see into the living room. Safa is sitting, knees to her chest right in front of the TV.

I check the message.

Beat.

"Feeling ill. Can't come out...?"

Beat.

I watch her for a few moments. Then I leave, closing the door quietly behind me.

ACT TWO

SAFA It's been a week. Everyone heads outside to observe the two minute silence. I walk alone. But I hear comments as I go past people.

"To hell with liberty."

"If you can't *live by the rules*, then you shouldn't be here. Simple as that."

"Sure, you can't blame everyone. But questions need to be asked. People need to *step up*."

AISHA The entire schools heads to the playground for the silence. I piece together bits of conversations the kids are having.

"But is it allowed?"

"Nah, the papers are just twisting things."

"Why blame all of us though?"

SAFA We stand in silence but I feel like my guilt is visible to the entire company. It's screaming out of me. It feels like those who share my religion are looking at me, as if to say, *this is shit for us*. And even those who look like us are saying, *thanks for this, life is going to be shit for us now too*.

AISHA Never seen them like this. Quiet and thoughtful. I hear sniffles... It's Sadia. I'm about to go to her but before I can, Tara puts her arm around her. It's like she just understands what's wrong.

SAFA In the lift we're all quiet. A few nods of acknowledgment. As we walk towards our desks, Helen tells me it's lucky I didn't come in that day. Then she turns to the others and they recall everything. And the comments don't stop.

"The police are just *doing their job*."

ACT TWO

"If you've got nothing to hide, then you've got nothing to fear."

"Everyone has to *adjust* right now and *understand.*"

AISHA Back in the classroom, I ask Sadia what's wrong. She tells me she heard about girls in Birmingham who had their scarfs pulled off their heads. And she's scared to walk home.

Beat.

And the girl's can't talk of anything else.

"My brother was stopped by police. He didn't even do anything."

"And they wonder why people are angry."

"They're making things worse for us."

Beat.

Why should anyone ever be scared like this?

SAFA I pick up a newspaper on the way to the station. I read the updates, hiding the pages as I do. From the corner of my eye, I notice a lady staring at me, before looking away and tutting.

I want to yell. *This is me trying to understand! I'm not one of them!*

Beat.

You can't explain guilt to everyone. I have a lot of experience with it. But this. It's the heaviest kind I've ever carried.

Beat.

How do you say sorry for something like this?

Lights change. A Thursday. SAFA*'s bedroom.*

AISHA *(reading a newspaper)* 'They look like the guys from uni don't they?'

SAFA 'Yeah.'

AISHA 'The girls in school can't stop talking about it. They're all scared and that.'

SAFA 'Why?'

AISHA 'Cos stuff's happening, innit. Scarfs being pulled off and that.'

SAFA 'Yeah, but why are they making it about themselves?'

AISHA 'They can't afford not to, I guess.'

SAFA 'We shouldn't be focusing on ourselves right now. It's selfish.'

AISHA 'It's not selfish. It's a reality. And if we want to understand/...'

SAFA '/Understand?'

AISHA 'So it doesn't happen again.'

SAFA 'Then we should *step up* by not making it about ourselves. *Live by the rules*. Then maybe it won't happen again.'

Beat.

AISHA 'I'm so glad you didn't go to work that day.'

SAFA 'God, why is everyone obsessed with that?'

AISHA 'What do you mean?'

SAFA 'Just don't say that to me, okay.'

AISHA 'Fine. I won't.'

Beat.

'Listen, don't let anybody give you shit. You don't owe anyone an explanation.'

SAFA 'We all owe explanations.'

AISHA 'Why are you talking so weird?'

SAFA 'Why are you getting so close to the kids? Never heard you talk about them like this before.'

AISHA 'Why shouldn't I?'

SAFA 'You're not there for long.'

AISHA 'So?'

SAFA 'They're gonna get attached to you.'

AISHA 'I doubt that.'

SAFA 'Yeah, they will. And that's not fair 'cos you're leaving soon.'

AISHA 'Well, you shouldn't get close to your work lot then either. You may not get the permanent job.'

Pause.

SAFA 'Listen I can't do next Thursday.'

AISHA 'Why not?'

SAFA 'There's a work event.'

AISHA 'When do you want to meet then?'

SAFA 'Any other day is fine.'

Beat

AISHA 'Fine.'

Lights change.

SAFA I've become more and more of an interest to everyone in the office.

"Where are you from, Safa?"

'Forest Gate. Near West Ham?' Yeah, they know.

"Yeah, but where are you *really* from?"

AISHA We're waiting in class for Tara, and the girls start asking *me* questions.

"Miss, why do they do it?"

'I don't know. But no one I've ever come across has said it's okay.'

They nod their heads.

SAFA "Do you support England or Pakistan when the cricket is on?"

"Are your parents progressive?"

"I had a Pakistani friend at university. Her parents were strict. But whose parents aren't strict, right?"

AISHA "My mum's scared even though I don't wear a scarf."

"My mum's scared even though I'm not Muslim."

"Miss, what does your mum say?"

Pause.

Images of Mum in her scarf run through my head. Memories mixed with pictures and stories of her to make her alive again.

Beat.

I know what she would say. So I tell them.

'She says never be scared of who you are.'

Lights change. A Thursday. SAFA*'s bedroom.*

'One of the girls, her brother was stopped by police twice on his way home. He came home really vexed.'

SAFA 'There's no need for that. Shouldn't get angry if he didn't do anything wrong.'

AISHA 'That's not the point.'

SAFA 'Yeah, it is. Police are just *doing their job*.'

AISHA 'What, to make people *feel* like they've done something wrong?'

SAFA 'Come on.'

AISHA 'Come on, what?'

SAFA 'Everyone has to *adjust* right now.'

AISHA 'It doesn't help. It's only making things worse.'

SAFA 'Is that what you say to them? Instead of telling them to be more understanding?'

AISHA 'I do whatever I can to help them. To make them feel better.'

SAFA 'If you want to help them, get them ready for the real world. Teach them how to *speak* properly. Tell them to explore outside the area.'

AISHA 'Why?'

SAFA 'Because we have to, okay. We just have to. Maybe things will change for the better soon. The Olympics being here. Maybe that will open up some doors for us.'

AISHA 'In what way?'

SAFA 'We don't talk to others, do we? We stay in our communities and we don't know other people.'

AISHA 'They don't know us either.'

SAFA 'How can they know us when we just stay with our own. We don't learn English. We don't think it's important.'

AISHA 'Who says it's not important?'

SAFA 'My mum, just as an example.'

AISHA 'Your mum can speak English.'

SAFA 'But she never needs to. Look around. When she goes to the shop to buy groceries, all the shopkeepers can speak Urdu or Punjabi or Hindi.'

AISHA 'So, what, she should go there and speak English to prove she can?'

SAFA 'No. That's not what I mean. You're not getting it.'

AISHA 'Your mum stays here because this is where they put us all. No one asked her to go off and try to find a job in another area. They didn't ask your dad or my dad. They told them to work in shitty little factories, right here. No one asked my mum to go teach in a different area when she was alive.'

SAFA 'It's up to us though isn't it? As individuals.'

AISHA 'Not everyone has that option.'

SAFA 'Not everyone chooses that option. They decided to stay put.'

AISHA 'And what's wrong with that?'

SAFA 'You're still here so you can't see it for yourself.'

AISHA 'So everything you're saying is a dig at me?'

SAFA 'Don't twist what I'm saying. You'll see when you start working in central too.'

AISHA 'I'm not twisting it. I'm trying to get to the point you're making.'

SAFA 'Okay. You chose to stay here. Even if we forgive our /parents...'

AISHA '/Forgive?'

SAFA '...for staying. We can choose to do things differently.'

Beat.

AISHA 'Wow.'

SAFA 'What?'

AISHA 'Nothing.

Pause.

'I'm really tired. I'm gonna go.'

Beat.

SAFA 'Fine.'

Lights change.

AISHA She's in one of her moods so I leave her to it.

Beat.

I get home and Dad is sleeping in front of the TV. The picture of Mum from the mantelpiece is next to him.

Beat.

Mum used to pray in that corner of the room, beads in hand. When she'd finish, she would blow on my face so gently.

Beat.

The day we buried her, I realised that it was too painful to even look at that corner again. So I didn't. And me and Dad, we couldn't look at each other in the same way again.

SAFA From the stairs, I can see Mum is sat on the edge of the sofa, waiting for the call to prayer. It's almost sunset. She's always prepared before time.

Beat.

Feels like such an event.

I'm about to go to her. But the call to prayer starts...and my legs stop.

AISHA I don't remember the last time I prayed. God left a gaping hole in my life, so why should I pray? I'm forced to see Him now though.

SAFA God feels like a mystery to me now. One night when I was six years old, it was thundering outside. I asked Mum why it thunders and she said, because God is angry. And I remember that even today whenever it thunders.

AISHA Dad never pressured me to pray, to fast, or even to think about God. But sometimes I wish he had given me some direction or something.

Beat.

I wonder what I'd believe if Mum was still here.

SAFA Whether it was the angry God or the God I pleaded with when I wanted to do well in exams. He was always there. I had never wondered what was and wasn't before. But now, I don't want to feel Him anymore.

Lights change.

AISHA Summer holidays are over like that. We're all sat in the staff room and, a few teachers from another department are across the room discussing how political the girls have become. Start saying that they have to watch out for any out of ordinary behaviour. I'm about to say something but Tara tells me to stay quiet. They won't get it even if I do.

SAFA Kim is putting me on a massive project with Helen. I'm shittin' it but Helen never hesitates in helping me. We go for coffee to talk about it and she's so complimentary of me. Says I work so hard and I'll be an asset to her for this. I hope I can live up to that.

AISHA Tara's talking to me about the PGCE again. Tell her I don't want to think about it right now. She knows what date is coming up.

Lights change. AISHA's *house.*

We do this every year but it never gets easier. Safa always spends the day with me, moving the sofas and coffee tables. Makes it easier for the next day.

Don't know why she's not here yet. No message from here either.

AISHA *starts to move things.* SAFA *arrives.*

SAFA 'Sorry there were delays. I literally spent the entire journey under someone's armpit.'

AISHA 'You were supposed to be here an hour ago.'

SAFA 'I know but the/ trains...'

AISHA 'You /should've told me you'd be late.'

SAFA 'I was underground.'

ACT TWO

AISHA 'So?'

SAFA 'There's no reception, Aisha.'

AISHA 'I'm having to do this myself. I could've asked someone else if you weren't going to show up.'

SAFA 'I'm here, Aisha. I'm late, but I'm here.'

AISHA 'There's so much to do.'

SAFA 'We know the routine. It doesn't take that long.'

AISHA 'It's not about that, Safa. I was expecting you. I need you to be here on time. Or don't bother coming at all.'

Beat.

SAFA 'I'm sorry. I'll let you know next time.'

Beat.

AISHA 'Let's just do this.'

They start clearing things. AISHA *takes out a large white cloth.*

'I'm sorry.'

Beat.

'Everything feels weird.'

Beat.

'I still miss her.'

SAFA 'I know. She'd be well proud of you though, y'know that?'

AISHA 'No, she wouldn't.'

SAFA 'Yeah, she would. You got a first. You're working. The girls look up to you. And you don't take crap from anyone.'

Beat.

'I wish I was like you.'

AISHA 'You are, Safa. Remember, you stood up to Faiza.'

SAFA 'I went and apologised later though.'

AISHA 'I know. She told me.'

SAFA 'When?'

AISHA 'I went to give her a smack for taking advantage of you.'

SAFA 'I should've known.'

Beat.

AISHA 'Come on, let's finish this. Then we can chill.'

They open the cloth and lay it out on the floor together.

Lights change. The next day.

I don't sleep. The next day comes around too fast.

Beat.

Ten years.

Beat.

Safa's always the last to leave. Dad tells her stories about Mum, but I think he's really telling me. We don't always talk about that stuff.

I help my aunt in the kitchen. She's been here all day. The house smells like when Mum used to cook.

SAFA Last day of the project. Been here 'til late everyday this week. But today is the one day I need to get out on time. I'm almost done. Three more emails to send and I can leave.

AISHA The room looks exactly like the day she died. I remember sitting here and watching my aunties and uncles move things around. Dad was sat quietly in a corner of the room. And then for days an endless number of people just came and went.

SAFA I'm about to grab my coat when Kim comes over. She needs me to photocopy some things.

Beat.

Okay, I can get this done in a few minutes.

AISHA At six o'clock the family start to come over. We all say a prayer. I usually hate this bit. But it's comforting today.

SAFA Fucking photocopier is jammed! I try to fix it but it keeps starting and stopping.

AISHA Dad starts his stories. For the first time, I sit next to him and listen. He's listing all the times Mum's old students have stopped him in the street to tell him how much confidence she gave them. He says she was a free spirit in a world of corpses.

SAFA I count the number of pages left to do. This is taking a lifetime. Aisha's going to be expecting me any minute.

AISHA And she was strong. He tells us about the time some skinheads pulled the scarf off her head when she was coming home from work. He wanted her to stop wearing it but she didn't. She refused to. Said… never be scared of who you are.

SAFA I put the copies on Kim's desk. I'm heading towards the lifts but Helen stops me. Tells me to stay for a few minutes 'cos they're celebrating the completion of the project. And they couldn't have done it without me.

Beat.

I can't say no.

AISHA I leave them talking and head upstairs. I walk into Dad's room. Mum's wardrobe is still full of her things. The things he can't throw away. Gathering dust. I rummage through and I think I can still smell her scent…

SAFA Tim gets us drinks. We gather around Kim's desk and she asks us what we'll have. I find myself getting nervous for some reason.

AISHA Her scarves are beautiful. Colourful. Warm. Just like she was. Whenever I'd hurt myself, she would blow into the corner of it and place it where the pain was. And I'd always feel better.

SAFA I should have said a coke or lemonade. But when Helen says wine, I find myself saying, 'the same.' There are surprised looks on people's faces. I think.

AISHA I take the most colourful one. Clearly from the seventies but retro patterns are back in fashion.

She puts the scarf on.

I look weird. I bet she looked much better with it on than me.

SAFA I watch how everyone drinks. Small sips. Not gulps. And they drink slowly.

AISHA I've seen plenty of those beehive looks around. Like Amy Winehouse's hair except it's fabric.

Holds the scarf up high.

Looks silly too. I try something else.

Wraps it around her head.

SAFA My tongue and neck burn. I feel my eyes go red as I try not to hurl. It's burning down to my chest.

AISHA Slightly bohemian. Not an easy thing.

She lets out a few strands of hair at the front.

SAFA I imagine Mum's face if she saw me now. I feel a different sort of guilt. It's harder to negotiate.

Beat.

I send Aisha a message.

AISHA Makes me feel a little more… feminine.

SAFA 'I can't make it.'

AISHA I wonder if I look like her now.

Lights change. The next day. AISHA's *house.*

SAFA 'I'm sorry.'

AISHA 'For?'

SAFA 'I got caught up at work. I thought I'd finish on time.'

AISHA 'Don't worry about it.'

SAFA 'Honestly, I was about to leave but Kim kept asking me to do things and then the printer wasn't working /and'

AISHA 'It's/ fine, Safa.'

SAFA 'Are you sure?'

AISHA 'Yeah.

Beat.

It's my fault really.'

SAFA 'What'd you mean?'

AISHA 'I told you not to come if you're not going to be on time. That's exactly what you did.'

Beat.

'You want to help or not?'

SAFA 'Yeah.'

They start to fold the large white cloth.

'How was it?'

AISHA 'Fine.'

SAFA 'What did your dad tell you?'

AISHA 'About?'

SAFA 'Your mum.'

AISHA 'Nothing.'

SAFA 'No new stories?'

AISHA 'No.'

SAFA 'Really? Did he retell them instead?'

AISHA 'No.'

SAFA 'Not even the really old ones?'

AISHA 'I said no, didn't I?'

SAFA *passes the folded cloth to* AISHA.

SAFA 'Aisha. I'm sorry. I swear I didn't realise how late it was going to get. You know I'd never miss this. Never have before. I especially wouldn't have missed it this year. You know that, right?'

Beat.

AISHA 'Yeah.'

They continue clearing up.

SAFA 'Honestly, we finished the project so last minute and then they said to stay for a drink and it got too late to come.'

AISHA 'You stayed for drinks?'

Beat.

SAFA 'I shouldn't have. I know. But I couldn't say no.'

Beat.

'I ended up trying some.'

AISHA 'You tried it?'

SAFA 'You were right. I feel so guilty. And I didn't want to come to your mum's khatam like that. I'm sorry, Aisha.'

Beat.

'Please say something.'

Beat.

'Please.'

ACT TWO

    Beat.

AISHA 'Do you want to go out?'

SAFA 'What?'

AISHA 'Get something to eat?'

SAFA 'Isn't there stuff leftover from yesterday?'

AISHA 'I feel like going out.'

    AISHA *picks up her scarf and puts it on.*

SAFA 'What are you doing?'

AISHA 'What?'

SAFA 'Why are you wearing that?'

AISHA 'Just.'

SAFA 'Where did you get it from?'

AISHA 'It was Mum's.'

SAFA 'Why do you have it on though?'

AISHA 'Why can't I have it on?'

SAFA 'Because you don't cover or practice.'

AISHA 'So? I like it. I think it looks good.'

SAFA 'Are you religious now?'

AISHA 'Why do I have to be religious to wear it?'

SAFA 'Isn't that how it usually works?'

AISHA 'Not always.'

SAFA 'So, start again. You just decided to wear it?'

AISHA 'Yeah.'

SAFA 'When?'

AISHA 'Last night.'

SAFA 'Why?'

AISHA 'I told you. Just.'

SAFA 'So what, you're going to stop drinking and smoking and clubbing now?'

AISHA 'No.'

SAFA 'Then why do you have it on?'

AISHA 'Why do you keep asking me?'

SAFA 'Because it's not you!'

AISHA 'It is me.'

SAFA 'Since when?'

AISHA 'Since I needed to prove who I am!'

Pause.

'I can clear the rest up myself.'

SAFA 'There's still so much to do.'

AISHA 'I can do it myself.'

Beat.

I walk out of the room and into the kitchen. I hear her footsteps. Maybe she's following me in.

Beat.

But a few moments later, the front door closes.

SAFA I don't go straight home. I take a few steps and then back to her house. I wait outside. Maybe she will come out in a minute.

Beat.

But she doesn't.

Light changes.

AISHA Dad is home early today. He sees me with the scarf on and something in his eyes tells me his mind is digging deep into memories. I freeze.

Beat.

But he smiles. Tells me I look just like Mum.

SAFA Mum tells me she saw Aisha at the khatam yesterday. Says she looks great with the scarf on. 'No, she looks like an idiot.' Her face drops. I go to my room and slam the door shut.

Light changes.

AISHA At school the girls take an interest in me wearing it. Ask me to show them how I styled it like that. Sadia asks me if I'm scared of wearing it, because of all the stories and that. I tell her, 'No, 'cos it's about being strong.'

SAFA Not long before my review. I schedule in half an hour with Helen to go over the questions. I stutter and stall and keep messing up but I'm grateful for her patience. She smiles and tells me to start again.

"Just be confident. You've done really well to be here."

She always seem to use a certain voice when she speaks to me.

AISHA When I see Tara, I tell her I've decided to apply for the PGCE. She's well proud.

SAFA I try to compose myself and start again and Helen tells me I shouldn't put this much pressure on myself.

"I know how difficult things must be for you at home. I've got some Muslim friends."

Beat.

I don't really understand why she said that.

Lights change.

New year and time for my review. I'm practically shaking. I sit with Kim and say everything I'd prepared. I speak slowly, confidently but I wish I could stop touching my face. When I finish, she congratulates me.

Beat.

I have a permanent job.

AISHA   The head of department wants to talk to all the teachers and TA's. He tells us the girls have become too political and we're required to keep an eye on them. Particularly the TA's. I listen but, 'I'm not doing that.' Tara tells me to keep quiet.

SAFA   Helen tells me how complimentary everyone is of me. I'm a pleasure to be around and always willing to help.

"There is one thing though."

My heart sinks.

"The scheme was temporary and there was no guarantee of you staying in the same post. We've hired within the company for your role but we were thinking, if it's okay with you, your demeanour is something we can still use in a junior post. You're so helpful. And you can apply for a promotion back to the post next year."

Beat.

I don't know what to say. I don't want to seem ungrateful.

'Okay'.

She smiles. And there's that voice again.

"Your parents must be so proud of you."

AISHA   Tara tells me that it may be best for me to take a break. Maybe find experience doing something else.

'This isn't about them is it? This is about choosing. You choose one or the other. And if that's the case, I know which side I'm on.'

I leave. On the way out, I see Sadia. She asks whether I'm coming to class.

Beat.

I don't know what to tell her.

Lights change. A Thursday. SAFA*'s house.*

SAFA 'You want to teach?'

AISHA 'Yeah.'

Beat.

SAFA 'I thought this was temporary?'

AISHA 'I changed my mind.'

SAFA 'And you're sure?'

AISHA 'Yeah.'

SAFA 'I'm really pleased for you, Aisha. I think you'll be…great.'

AISHA 'I know.'

Beat.

'How did your review go?'

SAFA 'It went well.'

AISHA 'You've been made permanent?'

SAFA 'Yeah.'

AISHA 'Ah, I knew you would!'

SAFA 'Thanks.'

AISHA 'Marketing Associate. High flyer and that.'

SAFA 'No, they kind of said that they think I'd be more useful in a different role.'

AISHA 'What role?'

SAFA 'Marketing Assistant.'

AISHA 'What about the Associate post?'

SAFA 'They've hired someone internally for that. But they said I can apply later this year.'

AISHA 'Why though?'

SAFA 'I'm more suited to this. I need a little more experience and that.'

AISHA 'But you've been doing that job since last year.'

SAFA 'Yeah, 'cos of the scheme though.'

AISHA 'Did they ever say that to you before though?'

SAFA 'No. But I assumed, which I shouldn't have.'

AISHA 'Safa. That ain't right. You earned that job. You deserve that job.'

SAFA 'It's the way it works. I can't do anything about it.'

AISHA 'How long are you going to keep saying that. It's the way it works, I can't do nothing about it. Aren't you sick of that?'

SAFA 'Why you getting so worked up? I've got a permanent job. That's what I wanted. So what is your problem?'

AISHA 'You deserved more than just a permanent role. You should've told them to stick it.'

SAFA 'Why do you do this? Why do you have to bring me down all the time?'

AISHA 'I'm trying to look out for you, Safa.'

SAFA 'I don't need you to look out for me, Aisha, okay. I'm not one of your students.'

Pause.

AISHA 'Okay, I'm sorry.'

Beat.

'I'm really happy for you, Safa. Honestly. I'm proud of you.'

SAFA 'Thanks.'

Beat.

'When are you sending your application?'

AISHA 'Deadline's midnight tomorrow.'

SAFA 'Want me to check it for you?'

AISHA 'If you want.'

SAFA 'I'll do it tomorrow, during lunch. Yeah?'

AISHA 'Yeah.'

SAFA 'Oh, hold on.'

SAFA takes out a small box and hands it to AISHA.

'Happy birthday.'

AISHA opens it.

AISHA 'Hoops.'

SAFA 'You can look all proper too.'

AISHA 'Thanks.'

SAFA 'You sure you don't want to go out?'

AISHA 'I don't feel like it. Just want to chill at home.'

Beat.

'Hey, I made a new playlist. Want to listen to it?'

SAFA 'Yeah.'

AISHA gets out her MP3 player. They put a headphone in each. A moment as they both enjoy the songs.[*]

AISHA 'D'you like it?'

SAFA 'Yeah, love it.'

---

[*] A licence to produce SPUN does not include a performance licence for any third-party or copyrighted music. Licensees should create an original composition or use music in the public domain. For further information, please see Music Use Note on page iii.

AISHA 'Take it. For your journey.'

Beat.

SAFA 'Aisha?'

AISHA 'Yeah?'

SAFA 'What do you think we'll be doing in ten years time?'

AISHA 'Why ten?'

SAFA 'Dunno. Random.'

Beat.

'Will we still be tight?'

Beat.

AISHA 'Yeah. I'll make sure of it.'

Beat.

SAFA 'Love you.'

Beat.

AISHA 'Shut up.'

Lights change. The next day. AISHA's *house.*

SAFA 'I don't understand why you did that. You said the deadline was midnight.'

AISHA 'You said you'd get to it at lunchtime.'

SAFA 'So, what? I got caught up. I said I was going to do it, didn't I?'

AISHA 'I didn't want to wait.'

SAFA 'I messaged you. I told you I'm having a late lunch but I'll get around to it.'

AISHA 'You said lunch yesterday. That's noon.'

ACT TWO

SAFA 'You can't understand for a second that I could be delayed. Instead you send it off before even giving me a chance.'

AISHA 'I gave you a chance. You didn't check it when you said you would. So I didn't wait.'

SAFA 'But I said to /you...'

AISHA 'Well/ I don't trust what you say anymore.'

Pause.

SAFA I really don't know what else to say to you then. I'll see you later.

Lights change. Time has passed.

AISHA I wake up to the sound of commotion outside. I get out of bed and pull back the curtains. I can't see anything though, so I head outside.

SAFA I come downstairs and Mum and Dad are staring at the TV screen. My brother is holding onto Mum's scarf.

"They raided a house. And shot a boy."

I recognise the street.

AISHA It feels like news commentary over images and videos of events. I could easily be at home seeing this on TV. That's how surreal it is. Everything is...

SAFA Chaos.

SAFA goes into a daze. Gets ready for work, putting her studs on. AISHA is watching the chaos.

ACT THREE

AISHA No charges for Forest Gate victims. But no apology yet. We all take to the streets with placards. Dad tells me Mum would've been leading this march if she was here.

SAFA I can hear the crowd from home. I sit down on the sofa and tell Mum I'm feeling unwell. She sits next to me. Puts her palm against my forehead. Her scent overwhelms me. I just want to curl up in her lap.

AISHA A lady approaches us with her young daughter. Dad recognises her. She hugs me and tells me she knew Mum. Says I look just like her.

SAFA I head upstairs. And the noise from outside just seems to follow me. I look from my bedroom window and everyone looks faceless from behind the net curtains. I pick them up from the corner.

Beat.

They look like a powerful army from here. I scan to see if I can see Mum and Dad.

AISHA We start walking slowly down these streets that are so familiar to us. But it all looks so different. There are photographers and cameras everywhere.

We follow the crowd down the side street next to Safa's house. I can see her window as we get closer. Feels weird not to be waiting for her. I wonder if she's in her room…

SAFA …But my eyes fall on her.

AISHA I see her! She sees me too. Someone in front gestures for her to come out. She drops the curtain and disappears.

ACT THREE

SAFA *sits on the floor. She doesn't move. She covers her ears.*

I know how it all must be happening in her house right now. She dropped the curtain so she can change her clothes. She's always in her pyjamas at home. She's going to put comfortable clothes on. Maybe her black joggers. And her black and silver trainers. She's going to put her jacket on and tell her mum that she's joining me for the march. And just as she's about to leave the house her brother's gonna say he wants to go too. But she's gonna say no because she knows that me and her will go for a milkshake after. She's going to come out any second now. Any second.

Beat.

She's going to be out any second now.

Lights change. Time has passed.

Safa's birthday today. I send her a text first thing. Sure I'm the first one to wish her. Like every year. Things haven't exactly been right with us lately, but she's still my best friend.

She picks up a small box.

Didn't get to give her her real present last year.

Beat.

It's perfect.

SAFA Helen insists on birthday drinks for me tonight. I wanted to spend the evening with Aisha, but I don't know if she'll want to. I tell her to come if she wants. I don't want to force her.

AISHA She sends me a text. She's having birthday drinks in this bar later. "Come if you want." Come if I *want*?

SAFA Helen, Kim and Tim are cracking jokes. I try my best to join in but I'm always hesitant. Cautious.

Tim turns to me, "So Safa, your family religious?"

'Yeah, very much so.'

AISHA I head to central, present in hand. I get there and find the bar they're all in. It's dim lights and noise. I look around and see Safa sitting with her colleagues.

SAFA I talk about the bombings for the first time. How disgusted I was. They listen. With a sort of glint in their eyes. When I finish,

"You're doing it right. The *normal* way."

"We have to *evolve* away from religion, right?"

"You're really *different*".

They all nod their heads, smiling, praising me for finding myself. Using that same voice again. I thank them. I don't really know how to respond.

AISHA *approaches.*

AISHA 'Safa.'

SAFA *(surprised)* 'Aisha?' You came?'

AISHA 'You invited me.'

SAFA 'Yeah.'

An awkward moment.

'Do you want to go outside?'

Lights change. A strange silence between them.

AISHA 'Got you something.'

AISHA *hands her the present.* SAFA *opens it to reveal a personalised pen.*

SAFA *(reads inscription)* 'For every great thing you do... It's beautiful. Thank you.'

Pause.

AISHA 'Enjoying your birthday drinks?'

SAFA 'Yeah. It's not bad.'

AISHA 'You having dinner with them too?'

SAFA 'Yeah, they said we'll go to that Portugeuse restaurant by the station.'

AISHA 'You get to do the posh restaurant thing then?'

SAFA 'Oh, yeah.'

Beat.

'I do.'

AISHA 'Is that wine?'

SAFA 'Sorry, can you smell it?'

AISHA 'A little. That was quick. Took me at least two years of drinking WKD before I even tried wine.'

SAFA 'Shall I get you a drink?'

AISHA 'Erm, no. I'm not sure I'm staying.'

SAFA 'Why not?'

AISHA 'I just wanted to give you your present.'

SAFA 'You came all this way just for that?'

AISHA 'I didn't know when I'd see you next.'

SAFA 'Aisha, you should've just popped to mine tomorrow then.'

AISHA 'Tomorrow?'

SAFA 'Yeah, tomorrow.'

AISHA 'Right. Tomorrow.'

SAFA 'What?'

AISHA 'Nothing. It's just. I always see you on your birthday.'

SAFA 'Yeah, but I feel bad that you came all this way.'

AISHA 'I just thought, it was something we do. Usually it's just the two of us, isn't it. But nice to have a proper party, innit.'

Pause.

'They seem... nice.'

SAFA 'Yeah. They are.'

AISHA 'Different.'

SAFA *'Different?'*

AISHA 'To the friends you've had before.'

SAFA 'Well, they're work friends.'

AISHA 'All this is different, isn't it?'

SAFA 'Yeah but, it feels... *normal* now.'

AISHA *'Normal?* As in... compared to what you're used to?'

SAFA 'It feels like, you know, I was in a bit of a bubble before.'

AISHA 'I don't know. This feels more like a bubble to me.'

SAFA 'You're not used to it, that's all.'

AISHA 'And you are?'

SAFA 'Yeah. I think.'

AISHA 'Right. Okay.'

Beat.

SAFA 'What is it?'

AISHA 'Nothing.'

SAFA 'There clearly is.'

Beat.

AISHA 'I don't know. I'm just trying to understand something. I mean break it down for me, Safa. You spend your whole life somewhere else but hanging around posh bars with posh people is normal for you?'

ACT THREE

SAFA 'Well, I don't know what you want to hear. It's just the way it is when you work here. You see things differently.'

AISHA 'And people differently too?'

Beat.

'You enjoying it?'

SAFA 'What?'

AISHA 'The drink.'

SAFA 'I'm getting used to it.'

AISHA 'Not used to it already?'

SAFA 'I don't know. Kind of.'

AISHA 'Would've thought you would be. You're in the right company. Often enough.'

SAFA 'What does that mean?'

AISHA 'Isn't it easier to get used to things when you have to... pretend.'

SAFA 'Pretend?'

AISHA 'Yeah. That you're used to it.'

SAFA 'Doesn't sound like you know what you're trying to say.'

AISHA 'Sorry. I'm not making myself clear?'

SAFA 'Clear. But not clear enough.'

AISHA 'Should I ditch the East London accent? You know, might make it easier for you to understand me. Now that you're so *well spoken* and that.'

SAFA 'I didn't say anything about the way you talk.'

AISHA 'It was just a few months ago that you spoke like me.'

SAFA 'So? Sometimes, you just have to... *evolve.*'

AISHA '*Evolve*? How much have you *evolved* then? I wonder if I can measure it. With a spoon maybe?'

SAFA 'What are you doing, Aisha?'

AISHA 'Nothing. I'm not doing anything.'

SAFA 'Yeah, you are. If you've got something to say, just say it properly.'

Pause.

AISHA 'Have you seen how much you've changed?'

SAFA *(scoffs)* 'You're wearing a scarf on your head.'

AISHA 'So?'

SAFA 'That's not you.'

AISHA 'I've told you why.'

SAFA 'It's still a change.'

AISHA 'Yeah, a superficial one. On the outside. But you've just. Changed. In every way.'

SAFA 'I haven't, okay. My life's just different now.'

Beat.

AISHA 'That's the first time you've said anything like that.'

SAFA 'Like what?'

AISHA '*My life*... Is this your *life* now? Is this the new you? The *real* you? Are you real in there with all of them or out here, with me.'

SAFA 'Can we just drop this. This is stupid.'

AISHA 'No. You owe me an explanation.'

SAFA 'For what? For wanting to achieve something more in my life.'

AISHA 'Like the rest of us aren't?'

SAFA 'I can't help it that you feel stuck. Stuck trying to figure yourself out. Well, sorry that I've grown up/.'

AISHA '/So pretentious.'

SAFA 'What the fuck does that mean?'

AISHA 'You haven't grown up. You've just discovered how to be something you're not.'

SAFA 'That's rich coming from you. With that thing on your head.'

AISHA 'It's called something.'

SAFA 'On your head, it's called being a hypocrite. You ain't no saviour to those girls, Aisha. Trying to get them to look up to you.'

AISHA 'I was your saviour though wasn't I? When you needed to be out late. When you needed someone to fight your battles. To tell your mum you're with someone. When you *needed* me.'

SAFA 'I thought that's what friends do. Didn't realise it was going to be thrown in my face at some point in the future.'

AISHA 'Friends? When is the last time you spoke to me?'

SAFA 'We texted yesterday.'

AISHA 'No, no. Not to tell me about plans. But actually *spoke* to me.'

Beat.

SAFA 'I've been busy.'

AISHA 'Busy for me. *Only* me.'

SAFA 'What do you want me to do? Drop everything?'

AISHA 'No, not everything. But don't drop me.'

SAFA 'I didn't drop you. Work came up.'

AISHA 'Your new life came up. Which is obviously too good for me to be a part of.'

SAFA 'Oh, stop feeling sorry for yourself, Aisha.'

AISHA 'I feel sorry for you. You think you fit in here?'

SAFA 'Don't talk to me about fitting in. You think you change your appearance and it makes you more like the girls in school?'

AISHA 'And you think socialising with them in there makes you like them? What a fake. You're not part of their bubble, Safa. You're outside looking in.'

SAFA 'Better than being just comfortable enough so you can just coast through life.'

AISHA 'Fuck you, Safa.'

AISHA *starts to walk off.*

SAFA 'No, no. Don't go. Let's hear your come back. Go on. Why don't you come inside with me? Come on. I want to see how well you do outside your comfort zone.'

AISHA 'I don't need to. They've already got their token Paki filling out some quota. Congratulations.'

SAFA 'And I guess the girls in school have found their pious leader. How would they feel if they knew who you really were?'

AISHA 'Who am I really?'

SAFA 'Tell them you drink. Just that one thing. Tell them.'

AISHA 'Sure. I will. Once you go in there and tell them about yourself.'

SAFA 'Tell them what?'

AISHA 'Go on. Tell them you're not some fucking victim. Your parents aren't honour killers. There are no terrorists in your family.'

SAFA 'They don't think that.'

AISHA 'That's what they see when they look at you. They're helping set you free without even knowing you.'

SAFA 'That's not what this is.'

ACT THREE

AISHA 'What is it then? That you're so *different* from the rest of us. That you're all superior because you're not that girl they think you're supposed to be.'

SAFA 'Well, guess that makes both of us then.'

AISHA 'I'm not trying to impress people like that who, despite everything, probably think I'm hiding a bomb under this.'

SAFA 'You might as well be.'

Beat.

AISHA 'What the fuck does that mean?'

SAFA 'You keep going down this road, then who knows.'

AISHA 'Yeah, real insightful of you. Because that's exactly how it works.'

SAFA 'How does it work then? You think you put a scarf on your head and all of a sudden you make up for all the years of hating everyone and everything around you? Well, it doesn't. You don't choose your side like that. That's not how it works.'

Beat.

AISHA 'When did you start hating yourself?'

SAFA 'That's rich coming from you?'

AISHA 'When did you start hating me then?'

SAFA 'Don't exaggerate.'

AISHA 'I must've done something though, right? Because you're not the same with me. Haven't been for ages.'

SAFA 'You're imagining it.'

AISHA 'You know when you didn't come to my mum's thing, you know what I thought?/'

SAFA 'I said sorry, Aisha/.'

AISHA '/I thought that maybe you were angry at me for something. Maybe I did something to upset you.'

SAFA 'I didn't mean to miss it. The whole project thing was going on.'

AISHA 'And you decided to stay and have drinks instead of be there for me.'

SAFA 'Just shut up, Aisha. Shut up!'

AISHA 'You know, I always thought the first time you'd try it would be with me. And I could look after you and we could have jokes together.'

SAFA 'We still can.'

AISHA 'You sure about that?'

Beat.

'What did I do, Safa? What did I do to make you so angry at me?'

Pause.

SAFA 'You made me bunk off. That's what you did.'

AISHA 'What?'

SAFA 'I should've been there that day. I should've been there.'

AISHA 'Why?'

SAFA 'So they could know I'm on their side. But I wasn't. I should've been there.'

Beat.

AISHA 'You shouldn't be trying to prove your side.'

SAFA 'You picked your side, didn't you? Well, so have I.'

AISHA 'Nah. You didn't pick it. It was picked for you. And you can't even see that.'

SAFA 'Just go home, Aisha.'

AISHA 'No. Not until you walk in there with me now.'

SAFA 'No.'

ACT THREE

AISHA 'Come on.'

SAFA 'No, I don't have to do anything.'

AISHA 'Come on, let's go.'

SAFA *(shouting)* 'I don't want to be seen with you! It's fucking embarrassing! You know how pathetic it is to see you trying to be all high and mighty now? Trying to get them kids to look up to you. Let me tell you something, Aisha. You are not your mum. And you're never going to be like her. So stop fucking trying!'

Pause.

AISHA 'I'm glad you have ambition. I'm glad you're getting somewhere in your life. But just remember. Doesn't matter how much you try to pretend. How much you try to change or forget the rest of us. To them in there, you will always be nothing more than a *smelly little oik*.'

AISHA *starts to walk off.* SAFA, *in a fit of rage, walks up behind her. She grabs her scarf and pulls it off. A few moments pass.* AISHA *doesn't take the scarf back. She walks off, leaving* SAFA *standing there with the scarf in her hand. Disbelief at what she just did.*

Lights change.

The sounds around are piercing me. Feels like everyone is shouting and the cars are driving towards me. I bump my way past faceless people. I don't even know where I am right now.

SAFA I follow the wall back towards the bar. I think I'm going to be sick. I'm not sure if I've come back to reality or left reality outside. Everything is just so... vivid.

Beat.

Smelly oik. That's all I am here.

Beat.

I grab my bag. I ignore Helen calling out after me. I run outside, past the shops, past the people, past the cars, the noise, the offices. I run and I run. My breath isn't catching. I feel like I'm going to faint.

Beat.

But she's gone.

Beat.

AISHA What's changed? We were hated then and we're hated now.

SAFA Except, we're starting to hate ourselves too.

EPILOGUE

SAFA 'Did you know, most people die close to where they grew up?

Beat.

'That's well scary, innit.'

AISHA 'Why?'

SAFA 'Cos both our birth and death certificates' are gonna say same thing.'

AISHA 'What they gonna say?'

SAFA 'London.'

AISHA 'No, they're not.'

SAFA 'What then?'

AISHA 'They're gonna say Newham.'

Lights fade. Blackout.

End

ABOUT THE AUTHOR

Rabiah Hussain is a playwright, poet and screenwriter from London.

Spun is Rabiah's debut full-length play, with runs in London, Montreal and Toronto. *Spun* was a finalist in the Best Stage Production category of the Asian Media Awards 2018.

In 2019, Rabiah was a writer for the Royal Court Theatre and Kudos TV Fellowship. In 2018, she was part of the BBC Drama Room scheme. Her monologue *Where I Live And What I Live For* had a run at Theatre Absolute in 2017, and her work has been part of programmes with Battersea Arts Centre, The Bunker Theatre, RADA, Rich Mix, The Space Arts Centre and Tamasha Theatre. Rabiah has completed writing programmes with Criterion Theatre, Hachette Publishing, Royal Court and Kali Theatre. She is an alumnus of the 2016 Tamasha Playwrights programme with Tamasha Theatre.

Rabiah has contributed published work to *Happy Birthday to Me: A collection of contemporary Asian writing* (Dahlia Publishing, 2010); *Hear Me Now: Audition Monologues for Actors of Colour* (Oberon, 2018); *Smashing It: Working Class Artists on Life, Art and Making It Happen* (The Westbourne Press, 2019) and *My White Best Friend And Other Letters Left Unsaid* (Oberon, 2020).

Milton Keynes UK
Ingram Content Group UK Ltd.
UKHW020642101123
432322UK00020B/952